POETRY

April 2018

FOUNDED IN 1912 BY HARRIET MONROE

VOLUME CCXII · NUMBER I

CONTENTS

April 2018

SPLIT THIS ROCK

BLACK GIRL MAGIC

SNOW CITY ARTS

Editor	DON SHARE
Art Director	FRED SASAKI
Associate Editor	LINDSAY GARBUTT
Assistant Editor	HOLLY AMOS
Marketing & Production Assistant	HANNAH KUCHARZAK
Consulting Editor	CHRISTINA PUGH
Design	ALEXANDER KNOWLTON
Design Consultant	PENTAGRAM

POETRYMAGAZINE.ORG

A PUBLICATION OF THE
POETRY FOUNDATION
PRINTED BY CENVEO PUBLISHER SERVICES

Poetry · April 2018 · Volume 212 · Number 1

Back in 1912, *Poetry*'s tiny first office was often crowded with visiting poets and friends, and founding editor Harriet Monroe would brew coffee over an open fire in an adjacent vacant lot. Visitors eventually would head out to a nearby restaurant where Monroe might buy lunch or dinner for writers down on their luck. Charming as this may sound, what she established all those years ago was what we would now call a poetry community. As Wallace Stevens once wrote, remembering Monroe, *Poetry* "was notably a magazine of many people ... in a group, she was always most eager." These days, poetry communities flourish everywhere, and stay in touch not only in person through readings and informal gatherings but moment to moment, via social media and texting.

In the spirit of such gregariousness, this month's issue presents work from three of many such active communities: Split This Rock, a gathering of those who work for social justice; *Black Girl Magic* — the name is self-explanatory, but these are poets connected to the BreakBeat poets featured in our April 2015 issue; and Snow City Arts, an organization that provides instruction in the visual arts, creative writing, music, theater, and media arts to children in hospitals. In juxtaposing work from each of these vibrant groups, we hope readers will get a sense of the vivacious energy and talent nourished wherever poets and their readers gather.

—*D.S.*

SPLIT THIS ROCK

Introduction

The thirteen poets gathered in this portfolio will read at Split This Rock Poetry Festival taking place April 19–21, 2018, in Washington, DC. Poetry — as ever — reminds us of what matters. When you're feeling particularly despondent — *Can it get any worse? Wait, it just did!* — I invite you to read these poems. They are community and beauty and mourning and fierce hope and resistance, all. They are restoration.

The poets are all ages, from their twenties to their eighties. Three have been role models to us in this work for decades and I want to take a moment to thank them profoundly, to say that we built Split This Rock on their shoulders. They are among the poets who inspire us as activists and writers, and who sustained us through the difficult years of struggling at the fringes of the literary landscape. They are Sonia Sanchez, Ellen Bass, and Sharon Olds.

Sonia Sanchez has been a lifelong activist for peace and justice and Black voices. She was a preeminent member of the Black Arts Movement and one of the earliest and most effective advocates for Black studies programs in higher education. She opened the first Split This Rock Poetry Festival by standing on a table in the middle of Busboys and Poets, a noisy restaurant and performance space in DC, invoking the ancestors and calling us all to use our powerful voices for justice.

Ellen Bass coedited, in 1973, the first major anthology of women's poetry, *No More Masks!*, a collection that ended the isolation of so many of us. When she was leading community writing workshops in the eighties she heard so many stories of childhood sexual abuse that she put her own writing on hold to focus on this horror and its healing. She produced one of the most essential texts on the topic, *The Courage to Heal: A Guide for Women Survivors of Child Sexual Abuse* (1988), which has sold over a million copies and has been translated into twelve languages. Bass's poems published here may not seem particularly political to some readers, but in their frank portrayal of LGBTQ family life and love one can find them profoundly political, disturbing as her vision of queer normalcy is to some.

Sharon Olds, in her eleven volumes of poetry, has freed millions of women from the shackles of shame that society has employed to control our bodies and thereby our minds and our very selves. Women's sexuality has always been policed, in every realm, including, of course, literature. Sharon Olds wrote the poems anyway; she stormed the gates. Additionally, over thirty years ago, she cofounded a program of writing workshops at a 900-bed state hospital for the severely disabled, at which she still teaches.

The poets in this portfolio represent some of the many stylistic strains of American poetry. They write lyrical, narrative, avant garde, formal, and elliptical work. The poets represent a range of racial, ethnic, religious, gender, and sexual identities. They have disabilities. Two — Paul Tran and Javier Zamora — are the children of US-exported wars, in Vietnam and El Salvador, respectively. They write achingly of the generational impact of war, violence, and forced migration on families, on psyches. Their poems, as do the others in the portfolio, remind us that all issues are connected: war and family violence, gender equity and economic disparity, immigration justice and the struggle to save our only home, this earth.

The poems challenge us — and they challenge us to ask the same of our government: what matters to us now, in 2018? What are we fighting for? What do we treasure enough to preserve, to bequeath to our children and our grandchildren?

Split This Rock was founded ten years ago precisely to promote the poems that ask these vital questions. A national organization whose mission is to cultivate, teach, and celebrate poetry that bears witness to injustice and provokes change, we've built Split This Rock from a single festival into a powerhouse, helping move this poetry from the margins to the center of our literary culture. The biennial national festival is our cornerstone program, but we also organize and present vibrant youth programs, an annual contest recently renamed the Sonia Sanchez-Langston Hughes Poetry Contest, the Freedom Plow Award for Poetry & Activism, readings, workshops, campaigns for social justice, a poem of the week series, and The Quarry: An Online Social Justice Poetry Database, housed on our website. We invite you to join us.

ILYA KAMINSKY

Question

What is a man?
A quiet between two bombardments.

Search Patrols

I cover the eyes of Gena, 7, and Anushka, 2,
as their father drops his trousers to be searched, and his flesh shakes,

and around him:
silence's gross belly flaps. The crowd watches.

The children watch us watch:
soldiers drag the naked man up the staircase. I teach his children's
    hands to make of anguish

a language —
see how deafness nails us into our bodies. Anushka

speaks to homeless dogs as if they are men,
speaks to men

as if they are men
and not just souls on crutches of bone.

Townspeople
watch children but feel under the bare feet of their thoughts

the cold stone of the city.

A Cigarette

Watch —
Vasenka citizens do not know they are evidence of happiness

in a time of war,
each is a ripped-out document of laughter.

God,
deaf have something to tell
that not even they can hear —

you will find me, God,
like a dumb pigeon's beak I am
pecking
every way at astonishment.

If you
climb a roof in the Central Square of a bombarded city, you will see
    my people and me —
one neighbor thieves a cigarette
another gives a dog
a pint of sunlit beer.

JAVIER ZAMORA

Guadalajara

We knew something was wrong when next to the TV, a large toma-
tillo plant was growing out the carpet. Everything there spoke, Table,
Lamps...

In the living room, Coffee Table's eyes glued to the TV: flags,
drums, hands on the chest on the screen, but it couldn't have been
Independence. It was the fifth of the fifth month, something about a
battle won, a battle lost.

Our host, Dining Table, handed each of us a green sphere. *Eat, s'il
vous plaît. Don't think about it*, she told us; then sent Chair and Coffee
Table to sleep.

Watch the bedbugs. You can't unlock the windows, Fan in the hallway
said.

For two weeks Table left tomatillos outside our door. The green
marbles punched through our stomachs, so deep, our ears grew roots.
It was as if no heat. Bed wished she was bigger. Closet dreaded his
clothes. Wall didn't let us sleep; kept saying,

*¡Look! Look over there, cabrones. You'll never make it there. If you're
gonna ask for the best route, the best price. ¿Where are your suspenders?
¿Dress shoes? You're not really serious about getting to San Francisco.
¿Are you? Pinche dirty pigeons.*

Whatever I Did After Has Not Happened Yet

at a certain time the kitten stopped moving I wanted to see if it would
    burn
    rain like cane fields when they're scorched after harvesting

through the phone Abuelita remembers the black kitten I threw in
    the fire
    still trying to crawl out that ash isn't snow Abuelo said shirtless

I picked up a mound in my hand if I look back at my front door
    barefoot kids in the street try catching the flakes on their tongues

come visit us they say nextyearnextyear I'll try again
    dust covers the roof my toys my hair my expired work permit burns

black the sky it is march again & again there's no wind
    Abuelita asks us to send a bag of autumn leaves she wants to keep

in a book the color so pretty interesting what if there's no wind
    I ask while acid at Joshua Tree camping the slight movements

of the twigs of the ocotillo sound like mice deep in their burrows
    with the silence of only this pen writing the only words I can hear

hella yellow now I'm in a similar dirt to Abuelita's yellow but here
    there's healing
    the cold the sky the same I'm staring at clouds the same

thought of then now again I could this could be the very cloud
    the very dirt but this time I'm happy yes I can be I'm smiling

The Master's House

To wave from the porch
To let go of the grudge
To disrobe
To recall Ethel Rosenberg's green polka-dotted dress
To call your father and say *I'd forgotten how nice everyone in these red
    states can be*
To hear him say *Yes, long as you don't move in next door*
To recall every drawn curtain in the apartments you have lived
To find yourself at 33 at a vast expanse with nary a papyrus of
    guidance, with nary a voice, a muse, a model
To finally admit out loud then *I want to go home*
To have a dinner party of intellectuals with a bell, long-armed,
    lightly-tongued, at each setting
To sport your dun gown
To revel in face serums
To be a well-calibrated burn victim to fight the signs of aging
To assure financial health
To be lavender sachets and cedar lining and all the ways the rich
    might hide their rot
To eye the master's bone china
To pour diuretic in his coffee and think this erosive to the state
To disrobe when the agent asks you to
To find a spot on any wall to stare into
To develop the ability to leave an entire nation thusly, just by staring
    at a spot on the wall, as the lead-vested agent names article by
    article what to remove
To do this in order to do the other thing, the wild thing
To say this is my filmdom, The Master's House, and I gaze upon it
    and it is good
To discuss desalinization plants and de terroir
To date briefly a banker, a lapsed Marxist, and hear him on the
    phone speaking in billions of dollars, its residue over the clear
    bulbs of his eyes, as he turns to look upon your nudity
To fantasize publishing a poem in the *New Yorker* eviscerating his
    little need

To set a bell at each intellectual's table setting ringing idea after idea,
and be the simple-footed help, rushing to say *Yes?*

To disrobe when the agent asks you to

To find a spot on any wall to stare into

To develop the ability to leave an entire nation thusly, just by staring
at a spot on the wall

To say this is my filmdom, The Master's House

To recall the Settler who from behind his mobile phone said *I'm
filming you for God*

To recall this sad God, God of the mobile phone camera, God of the
small black globe and pixelated eye above the blackjack table at
Harrah's and the metal, toothed pit of Qalandia checkpoint the
same

To recall the Texan that held the shotgun to your father's chest,
sending him falling backward, pleading, and the words came to
him in Farsi

To be jealous of this, his most desperate language

To lament the fact of your lamentations in English, English being
your first defeat

To finally admit out loud then *I want to go home*

To stand outside your grandmother's house

To know, for example, that in Farsi the present perfect is called the
relational past, and is used at times to describe a historic event
whose effect is still relevant today, transcending the past

To say, for example, *Shah dictator bude-ast* translates to *The Shah was
a dictator*, but more literally to *The Shah is was a dictator*

To have a tense of is-was, the residue of it over the clear bulb of your
eyes

To walk cemetery after cemetery in these States and nary a gravestone
reading *Solmaz*

To know no nation will be home until one does

To do this in order to do the other thing, the wild thing, though
you've forgotten what it was

The End of Exile

As the dead, so I come
to the city I am of.
Am without.

To watch play out around me
as theater —

audience as the dead are audience

to the life that is not mine.
Is as not
as never.

Turning down Shiraz's streets
it turns out to be such

a faraway thing.

A without which
I have learned to be.

From bed, I hear a man in the alley
selling something, no longer by mule and holler
but by bullhorn and jalopy.

How to say what he is selling —

it is no thing
this language thought worth naming.
No thing I have used before.

It is his
life I don't see daily.
Not theater. Not play.

Though I remain only audience.

It is a thing he must sell daily
and every day he peddles

this thing: a without which

I cannot name.

Without which is my life.

CAMILLE T. DUNGY

Naming what has risen

Why not a crocus from this bulb? Why not the purple
of bees' lust so that, in honey, she might taste something
good? Under skin, purple is a private taste, closer
to the blood of her tongue, closer to the blood
she chokes on when she's gasping, to the clot
behind her blackened eye. The heated force
that slammed her shin, that pushed bone
from the bone, that arched her but did not
approach caress, is another kind of lust. Spring:
a madness of grappling. Isn't that what she sees outside
every window? And inside? Nothing unique going on.

this beginning may have always meant this end

coming from a place where we meandered mornings and met quail, scrub jay, mockingbird, i knew coyote, like everyone else, i knew cactus, knew tumbleweed, lichen on the rocks and pill bugs beneath, rattlers sometimes, the soft smell of sage and the ferment of cactus pear. coming from this place, from a place where grass might grow greener on the hillside in winter than in any yard, where, the whole rest of the year, everything i loved, chaparral pea, bottle brush tree, jacaranda, mariposa, pinyon and desert oak, the kumquat in the back garden and wisteria vining the porch, the dry grass whispering long after the last rains, raccoons in and out of the hills, trash hurled by the hottest wind, the dry grass tall now and golden, lawn chairs, eucalyptus, everything, in a place we knew, every thing, we knew, little and large and mine and ours, except horror, all of it, everything could flame up that quickly, could flare and be gone.

Scientific Method

Of course I chose the terry cloth surrogate. Milkless
artifice. False idol. Everyone, I'm told, has a mother,

but Master bred me in a laboratory, his colony
of orphans. Rhesus macaque. *Macaca mulatta*. Old
World monkeys, my matriarchs ruled the grasslands

and forests long before white men like him weaned
their whiteness and maleness from our chromosomes,

slashed and burned our home, what they once called
The Orient. French Indochina. Việt Nam. Master,
like a good despot, besotted and dumbstruck, dying

to discern the genesis of allegiance, the science of love
and loss, nature versus nurture, segregated me at birth

from my maker, pelt sopping with placental blood.
In a chamber where he kept track of me, his pupils
recorded my every movement, my every utterance,

hoping I might evince to them a part of themselves.
But I wasn't stupid. I knew famine and emaciation,

and nevertheless I picked that lifeless piece of shit
because it was soft to hold. Who wouldn't want that?
Though it couldn't hold me, I clung to the yellow-face

devil as though it was my true mother and I grasped
the function of motherhood: witness to my suffering,

companion in hell. Unlike infants with wire mothers
I didn't hurl myself on the floor in terror or tantrum,
rocking back and forth, colder than a corpse. I had

what Master believed to be a psychological base
of operations. Emotional attachment. Autonomy.

Everything he denied and did to me, his ceaseless
cruelty concealed as inquisition, unthinkable until
it was thought, I endured by keeping for myself

the wisdom he yearned to discover and take credit
for. Love, like me, is a beast no master can maim,

no dungeon can discipline. Love is at once master
and dungeon. So don't underestimate me. Simple-
minded and subservient as I might appear to be,

I gathered more about Master than he did
about me, which, I guess, is a kind of fidelity

conceived not from fondness but fear magnified
by fascination. Master made me his terry cloth
surrogate, his red-clawed god, nursing his id

on my tits, and for that, I pitied him. All this time
he was the animal. All this time he belonged to me.

SHARON OLDS

Poem Which Talks Back to Itself

For Etan Patz

The parents whose boy went off to school
that morning — the police may have found someone
who saw their son, alive, after
they saw him for the last time. *Step away!*
Someone who saw that elfin face
change, at the word "soda." *Step back!*
And change again, and change. And down
the basement steps, down into the earth,
the stairs down into the underworld.
Don't go there. Close your eyes. Someone
may know the unbearable — someone
in custody. O, "custody."
A wall of dirt, a wall of stone,
a bare bulb, like the uterus upside
down. No Kaddish, no washing of the dead,
no linen shroud, no company
through the long night.
Whatever honor can be kept for him —
his pure and whole honor is kept
by his parents, for the rest of the hard
labor of their lives. All this time,
they could not die, so they'd be here, in case
he came back. *Unspeakable.* And now,
the one taken in for questioning cries out,
"I don't know why, I don't know why."
He will not tell. Is he holding that hour
to himself. Did he hold that child in his hands,
39 years ago.
Vanished. The spirit mattered away.
And the dear matter — *don't.* The bag,
the truck. The landfill or the barge, the burial
at sea — the dispersal, the containment within
the bounds of the oceans, crested on top and

cragged at the floor where the innards of the planet pour
up, molten, through fissures — contained
in the air bound by the atmosphere, the
clouds of mourning pressing against
the inner surface of the casing. *Shut
your mouth. Put down your pen. Drop
your weapon! Stop! In the name of the law
and the prophets.* At his birth, the history of the earth began.

How It Felt

Even if I still had the clothes I wore,
those first twelve years, even if I had
the clothes I would take off before my mother
climbed the stairs toward me: the glassy
Orlon sweater; the cotton dress,
under its smocking my breasts-to-be
accordion-folded under the skin of my chest;
even if I had all the sashes,
even if I had all the cotton
underwear, like a secret friend,
I think I could not get back to how
it felt. I study the stability
of the spirit — was it almost I who came back
out of each punishment,
back to a self which had been waiting, for me,
in the cooled-off pile of my clothes? As for the
condition of being beaten, what
was it like: going into a barn, the animals
not in stalls, but biting, and shitting, and
parts of them on fire? And when my body came out
the other side, and I checked myself,
10 fingers, 10 toes,
and I checked whatever I had where we were
supposed to have a soul, I hardly dared
to know what I knew,
that though I had been taken down,
again, hammer and tongs, valley
and range, down to the ground of my being
and under that ground, it was possible
that in my essence, at the center of my essence, in some
tiny chamber my mother could not
enter — or did not enter — I had not been changed.

SONIA SANCHEZ

Haiku and Tanka for Harriet Tubman

1

Picture a woman
riding thunder on
the legs of slavery...

2

Picture her kissing
our spines saying *no* to
the eyes of slavery...

3

Picture her rotating
the earth into a shape
of lives becoming...

4

Picture her leaning
into the eyes of our
birth clouds...

5

Picture this woman
saying *no* to the constant
yes of slavery...

6

Picture a woman
jumping rivers her
legs inhaling moons ...

7

Picture her ripe
with seasons of
legs ... running ...

8

Picture her tasting
the secret corners
of woods ...

9

Picture her saying:
You have within you the strength,
the patience, and the passion
to reach for the stars,
to change the world ...

10

Imagine her words:
Every great dream begins
with a dreamer ...

11

Imagine her saying:
I freed a thousand slaves,
could have freed
a thousand more if they
only knew they were slaves ...

12

Imagine her humming:
How many days we got
fore we taste freedom ...

13

Imagine a woman
asking: *How many workers*
for this freedom quilt ...

14

Picture her saying:
A live runaway could do
great harm by going back
but a dead runaway
could tell no secrets ...

15

Picture the daylight
bringing her to woods
full of birth moons...

16

Picture John Brown
shaking her hands three times saying:
General Tubman. General Tubman. General Tubman.

17

Picture her words:
*There's two things I got a
right to: death or liberty* ...

18

Picture her saying *no*
to a play called *Uncle Tom's Cabin*:
I am the real thing ...

19

Picture a Black woman:
could not read or write
trailing freedom refrains...

20

Picture her face
turning southward walking
down a Southern road ...

21

Picture this woman
freedom bound ... tasting a
people's preserved breath ...

22

Picture this woman
of royalty ... wearing a crown
of morning air ...

23

Picture her walking,
running, reviving
a country's breath ...

24

Picture black voices
leaving behind
lost tongues ...

ELIZABETH ACEVEDO

Iron

And although I am a poet, I am not the bullet;
I will not heat-search the soft points.

I am not the coroner who will graze her hand
over naked knees. Who will swish her fingers

in the mouth. Who will flip the body over, her eye a hook
fishing for government-issued lead.

I am not the sidewalk, which is unsurprised
as another cheek scrapes harsh against it.

      Although I too enjoy soft palms on me;
enjoy when he rests on my body with a hard breath;
                            I have clasped
this man inside me and released him again and again,
listening to him die thousands of little deaths.

What is a good metaphor for a woman who loves in a time like this?

I am no scalpel or high thread count sheet. Not a gavel, or hand-
    painted teacup.
I am neither   nor romanced by the streetlamp nor candlelight;
my hands are not an iron, but look, they're hot, look
how I place them   in love   on his skin
and am still able to unwrinkle his spine.

Atlas

If you open up any atlas
and take a look at a map of the world,
almost every single one of them
slices the Pacific Ocean in half.
To the human eye,
every map centers all the land masses on Earth
creating the illusion
that water can handle the butchering
and be pushed to the edges
of the world.
As if the Pacific Ocean isn't the largest body
living today, beating the loudest heart,
the reason why land has a pulse in the first place.

The audacity one must have to create a visual so
violent as to assume that no one comes
from water so no one will care
what you do with it
and yet,
people came from land,
are still coming from land,
and look what was done to them.

When people ask me where I'm from,
they don't believe me when I say water.
So instead, I tell them that home is a machete
and that I belong to places
that don't belong to themselves anymore,
broken and butchered places that have made me
a hyphen of a woman:
a Samoan-American that carries the weight of both
colonizer and colonized,
both blade and blood.

California   stolen.
Samoa   sliced in half   stolen.
California, nestled on the western coast of the most powerful
country on this planet.
Samoa, an island so microscopic on a map, it's no wonder
people doubt its existence.
California, a state of emergency away from having the drought
rid it of all its water.
Samoa, a state of emergency away from becoming a saltwater cemetery
if the sea level doesn't stop rising.
When people ask me where I'm from,
what they want is to hear me speak of land,
what they want is to know where I go once I leave here,
the privilege that comes with assuming that home
is just a destination, and not the panic.
Not the constant migration that the panic gives birth to.
What is it like? To know that home is something
that's waiting for you to return to it?
What does it mean to belong to something that isn't sinking?
What does it mean to belong to what is causing the flood?

So many of us come from water
but when you come from water
no one believes you.
Colonization keeps laughing.
Global warming is grinning
at all your grief.
How you mourn the loss of a home
that isn't even gone yet.
That no one believes you're from.

How everyone is beginning
to hear more about your island
but only in the context of
vacations and honeymoons,

football and military life,
exotic women exotic fruit exotic beaches
but never asks about the rest of its body.
The water.
The islands breathing in it.
The reason why they're sinking.
No one visualizes islands in the Pacific
as actually being there.
You explain and explain and clarify
and correct their incorrect pronunciation
and explain

until they remember just how vast your ocean is,
how microscopic your islands look in it,
how easy it is to miss when looking
on a map of the world.

Excuses people make
for why they didn't see it
before.

SHERWIN BITSUI

From "Dissolve"

On limbs of slanted light
painted with my mind's skin color,
I step upon black braids,
oiled, drenched, worming
from last month's orphaned mouth.

Winged with burning —
I ferry them
        from my filmed eyes, wheezing.

Scalp blood in my footprints —
my buckskin pouch filling
        with photographed sand.

No language but its rind
        crackling in the past tense.

•

Tearing apart cloud names —
pierced fog commands:
douse the inferno's ribs
with opaque forgetting;
clip dawn from the book's dusk,
unfasten the song's empty auditorium
        over a garden of mute foals.

Tearing apart fog names —
pierced cloud sings:
let them shriek from their hinges,
let them slice their gills open
with flint knives
and circle their ghosts
as frog-skinned antelope,
let them drag their legs over a trail
anchored to a ladder
that has soaked up blood
since land began crawling out of anthills.

·

Slipping into free fall,
we drip-pattern: *the somewhere parts,*
our shoulders dissolving
                            in somewhere mud.

The arcing sun whistles
across the mask's abalone brow,
its blurring pouts into a forest
chirping from a lake's bite marks
stamped vertically on this map's windowsill.

Kneeling our thoughts on ellipses
evaporating from ollas of fragrant wet clay —
we saddle the drowning's slippery rim.

From "The Voice of Sheila Chandra"

What represses unhomes in the sound
Who has made me what is made me
Is a voice just muscles and shape and
Breath to phrase a song boats assemble
At the mouth of the harbor mouth in
Earth you who wrote an ode to silence
Never wrote of what is silenced I did
Seek all resounding caves let the voice
Be lit all the lanterns in the new world we
Need the language of stone from string
To string quiver in the opening the garden
So beautiful Lucifer dark sun of morning
No Eden but innocence no expulsion
But after

•

No more will I listen to other than
A single note moaned not known
I do not here think again what place
Presents itself own moan well eye
Here body as a battery of the one
Moment when it is time to open
Your mouth to plug in I will allow what
I invented to find its color make
A shape which neither water nor
Sky do how do you now in this
Contained shape go through
Your life not like a constellation
Not guessed at intuited or divined
No name so how do you discern a shape for
What is often called g-d

•

Vantablack was made for missiles
Or planes for defense purposes so dark
No eye could see it some voices are
Like that no one could hear them it
Is not good to be lost to be lost is
More than metaphor for spiritual
Condition I sit at the terrace overlooking
The green sea perhaps it is failure
That ought to be sought the voice
That fails falls silent Sheila's or
The body's the blue failed me the sun
Fails every evening I we you have all
Failed too everyone who strove all these
Long years for peace failed

•

August 7 Predawn blue and blue the sound
Of the sea further away and less violent lights
On the water fishing boats closer than I
Imagined no one is awake some animals
Maybe what I do without knowing in a
Harrowing world what I do without knowing
As I listen to the gurgle of water against
The promontory I feel like I am listening
To a body how slow and opening a piece
Of tune where one does not know how
It will unfold no chord or cadence to tell
You in sound what the path will be how
It will happen until it happens I do not want
To be alone what does it mean anyway when
Someone says "Muslim"

•

Can she still feel music in her body can she
Vocalize even without technology of the
Mouth tongue palate glottis vocal chords
What is a voice Anish Kapoor granted
Exclusive right to work with blackest
Black she now communicates through notes
And gesture Vantablack made for
Military purposes like sound also used
For torture all sounds to wake you vibrate
Your brain what emerges as an echo from
Music as torture children on the beach
Playing god is sound or art or science
Shit and sex the body's echo what mess
Is left in the big or the little death

•

Sheila's voice always in the background
Always disappearing into the music
Of what surrounds it the way one loses
Oneself in sex or death or the moment
Of shitting I got lost in Salman's
Music he said it was a surrender of
Ego when he left me behind but really
It was a surrender of my will words too
Have god inside but for the prize of
The body they do not compete can
Not hold the storm of time cannot
Hold the line do I touch the ocean
Inside will my family come to
My funeral

•

That night we swam the full moon
Civilized us federated us gave us
Our nationality we who were lost
I have now lost what little heritage
I did have returned to the rude
Rough world long vowels of
Morning evening birds scream
No soft blanket falling to cover
But a throttling a suffocation
Of dusk no silence when the self
Stills the absence of noise is itself
Torture I cannot sleep tongued loose
Drones move through a riff by
A singer without papers

●

August 9 Eleanna takes me out on
The water Miller exploding the form
Of the novel itself I see now how Nin
Wanted to move away from his vociferous
Singing of the world as material to try
To construct a music of the way
The mind works still fed by light on the
Water a mute noise of engines under
Water as the boat passes the light
House and heads out for open sea
Remembering in Palestine crawling
Down the hill trying to catch a wifi
Signal from the settlement untapped
Improvisation of space

●

At the stone terrace the gardener lingers
Clipping hedges while I work breeze
Between us soon I will return I read
The article about a poet who was killed
In the street his poems untranslated
All the artists and writers killed the open
Space of the sea yesterday Eleanna and I
Went too far out went almost all the way
To Marseille we saw the pink-gray sky
Of wildfire I accepted the waves I found
In the chapters of the Quran to sing my
Way through turbulence draw a way
Through the waves savage wildfire all
The villages evacuated

•

We woke to the smell of burning air
A little cool smell of charred refuse
Colors muted last night the moon
Came clear nearly blue eyes too
Painfully large rough on the eyes and
Impatient but I wanted to look so
Badly for the meteors the sea
Crashing against the rocks smoke
From the fire obscured the sky
In the morning we rowed across
The harbor and realized fear of heights
And fear of depth is the same just one
You see and one you don't

Marriage

When you finally, after deep illness, lay
the length of your body on mine, isn't it
like the strata of the earth, the pressure
of time on sand, mud, bits of shell, all
the years, uncountable wakings, sleepings,
sleepless nights, fights, ordinary mornings
talking about nothing, and the brief
fiery plummets, and the unselfconscious
silences of animals grazing, the moving
water, wind, ice that carries the minutes, leaves
behind minerals that bind the sediment into rock.
How to bear the weight, with every
flake of bone pressed in. Then, how to bear when
the weight is gone, the way a woman
whose neck has been coiled with brass
can no longer hold it up alone. Oh love,
it is balm, but also a seal. It binds us tight
as the fur of a rabbit to the rabbit.
When you strip it, grasping the edge
of the sliced skin, pulling the glossy membranes
apart, the body is warm and limp. If you could,
you'd climb inside that wet, slick skin
and carry it on your back. This is not
neat and white and lacy like a wedding,
not the bright effervescence of champagne
spilling over the throat of the bottle. This visceral
bloody union that is love, but
beyond love. Beyond charm and delight
the way you to yourself are past charm and delight.
This is the shucked meat of love, the alleys and broken
glass of love, the petals torn off the branches of love,
the dizzy hoarse cry, the stubborn hunger.

I Could Touch It

When my wife was breaking apart, my son was falling in love.

She lay on the couch with a heated sack of rice on her belly,
sometimes dozing, sometimes staring out the window at the olive tree

as it broke into tiny white blossoms, as it swelled into bitter black fruit.

At first, I wanted to spare him.
I wished he was still farming up north, tucking bulbs of green onions
into their beds and watering the lettuce,
his hands gritty, his head haloed in a straw hat.

But as the months deepened, I grew selfish.

I wanted him here with his new love.
When I passed the open bathroom door, I wanted
to see them brushing their teeth,

one perched on the toilet lid, one on the side of the tub,
laughing and talking through their foamy mouths,
toothbrushes rattling against their teeth.

Like sage gives its scent when you crush it. Like stone
is hard. They were happy and I could touch it.

KWAME DAWES

Ode to the Clothesline

After Alfred Stieglitz

Not so much the missing of things
but the nostalgia of colors, their music,

the ordinary revelation of a family's life
caught in the flop and dance, a jig,

if you will, of their layers, outer and inner skins,
the secret things so close to the body,

the taste, the salt and sweet of blood, and shit,
and piss, and then, rinsed and scrubbed, leaving

beneath the astringent scent of soap
a musky marker of self for strays

to smell or imagine as they walk
past the parade of the living

on taut lines, propped by poles
with nails for a hook, above

the startling green of grass and hedge,
the barefaced concrete steps,

the sky, inscrutable as a wall;
this is what one carries as a kind

of sweetness — the labor of brown hands,
elbow-deep in suds, the rituals

of cleansing, the humility of a darning
or a frayed crotch, the dignity

of cleanliness, the democracy of truth,
the way we lived our lives in the open.

Vagrants and Loiterers

South Carolina, c.1950

You got that clean waistcoat,
the bright white of a well-tailored
shirt, you got those loose-as-sacks
slacks and some spit-polished shoes,
and you know, whether you are looking
like money, or about to take a stroll,
to tilt that hat like you own
the world; yeah, smoke your pipe,
roll your tobacco, and hold loose
as authority, your muscles, lithe
and hard; and every so often, when
you feel the urge, you reach into the waist
pocket and pull out that watch on its
chain, then look in the sky and say
Gonna be a cold one when it come,
like God gave you that fancy clock
to tell the future. These are the easy
boys of the goodly South; waiting for
what is out of frame to happen:
the sheriff with his questions, the
paddy wagon, the chain gang, the weight
of the world. Waiting, with such delicate
dignity, fickle as the seasonal sky.

BLACK GIRL MAGIC

MAHOGANY L. BROWNE

On Black Girl Magic

My sister-in-law, who I call my Sister, is what most would like to call a "firecracker." She married my youngest brother, born to a father who was married to my mother lifetimes before, and we've been kin ever since. Whatever she says, it's usually with a snap of her eyes, a cut of her lips, or a finger wag. It is not a performance of blackness — she is a Black woman. And these movements are hers, just like they were her mother's. Just like they were her grandmother's. A tradition of survival. She's learned how to get her point across neatly: a knife in a drawer full of spoons. She's always accused of being too "rough" on people. Which is where our sisterhood thickens, molasses strong.

I too have lived on that block, in that house, first door to the right and you could find me: Angry Black Girl/Strong Black Girl/Black Girl You Call On When You Need to Get Things Done.

My Sister, T, is too this woman; unapologetically, listening to Beyoncé with her three Black daughters and her eldest Black son. Praying faithfully for forgiveness, because she's begun to believe that she is hard to love. T, who snaps her eyes when pointing across the room, need not pray for forgiveness, I say. But it's hard to believe someone like me, especially when the world is fixed on telling her how strong and loud and wrong she is. I introduce to her June Jordan's mantra *"I am not wrong: Wrong is not my name"* and we weep a little between laughter. There are these moments that I hold close to my chest. The phone glued to my ear as we cackle between shit talk and ferocious laughter.

Where in the world do they love a Black Girl for being herself? We are primed to bear witness to Kardashians and Jenners pretending to be Black women with their cornrows and Black boyfriends, their acrylics beaming under the hot light, the world their stage. No one asks them to settle down their finger snaps or tone down their hair color. No one judges them for their sexual partners or the sex tapes that leak. Their children are born, revered as beautiful, receive rightfully the world's love. They are offered modeling contracts and makeup deals like candy, as we sit by idly, college tuition debt growing, as our children die from lead poisoning in Flint or with a handful of skittles in Florida or because of disobedience in Maryland or sleeping quietly on the family couch in Michigan.

Where in the world do they love a Black Girl for being herself? Where a twenty-seven-year-old activist can die after her second child is born due to cardiac arrest. Her weight and height and eating patterns are blamed for her health, never the stress it must've caused her heart to watch her father ripped from this earth, on repeat in hi-def display; a reminder that Black death is the only thing certain and ours. Her name, so closely linked to the ghost of her father, Erica; a chant no one will sing until she is gone. My sister, T, is not my blood sister. But she is mine. She is me. We are one and the same when we love how we love. Our teeth bared and gleaming because we've grown to understand "I love you" as a weapon held against our throats. We retreat into ourselves and fight others who are trying to kill us: family members, friends, neighbors, and supervisors. We understand the small deaths (TV shows where all you see are jokes about us; weaves overpriced and deemed out of style until a hashtag with Gigi, the newest trendsetter, mimics a Black girl from IG; or the men we love disposing of us with statements of "too much" falling from their open palms) can culminate into an ultimate death. A death where there is no room for the love of ourselves, beginning the journey of void-filling through addiction, dangerous surgeries, and loneliness. Though we oftentimes find ourselves unfolding to protect those same hands during vigils, protests, and rallies. This is what Black women have been taught to do. Love and show up for what love has survived. And so, we do. Let those that look like us take from us, until there is nothing left. We understand we are the backbone despite the backhand. And we love with the harshest tongues, believing that the survivors of such a spectacle are here to stay. We share intimacy this way, in hopes that if you see combat deserving of affection, maybe you too will swing in the protection of our names.

But this is not a fail-proof plan. This is not the blueprint for home. For many years, I believed it was our only heirloom. To speak as hard as you love. I spoke to T today. I told her about the importance of apologizing. She sighs and cuts me off: "I meant it, Sister, I'm not sorry." And I hear me ten years before, angry and seething and righteous. I reply: "It's not about being right. You are not apologizing for what you believe to be true, you are apologizing for your hand in hurting someone else."

We hang up soon after and I am spinning because while I ask my Sister to do things I wasn't capable of doing at her age, I wish someone had told me about the power of forgiving myself. I believe we have the right to be snarky and witty and throw shade, if we choose. We owe ourselves the right to speak through a world that's tried to mute us all of our lives. But I know the difference between intention and impact. We've seen this before. And so we lash out, because we know our very lives are in danger. Zora Neale Hurston wrote, "If you are silent about your pain, they'll kill you and say you enjoyed it." Eleanor Bumpers, Korryn Gaines, Tanisha Anderson, Yvette Smith, Miriam Carey, Malissa Williams, Sandra Bland, and Rekia Boyd: killed for standing up, sitting down, speaking back, protecting their children, or just being Black women.

I believe with my whole self: ain't no room for a Black woman's voice to be policed. Our worth is always up for debate. My Sister is one of the kindest women I know. I have witnessed her crumble to the ground in fear for her child and reach into her deepest pocket for grace when dealing with the gracelessness. Black women are often asked to lead (silently) and be the symbol of civility while everyone else plays from a different rulebook, mocking their existence the entire time. T is the woman I dreamed of becoming. The way she rides for my little brother — their marriage is a fortress of forgiveness and love, the way it stretches until there is room for all of their children and their dreams. T sends me a text about being hard to love and I want to cry. Such a folktale: being hard to love. What a fable we've grown to believe as the rule. T is so easy to love. We are so easy to love. Our resilience and expansion is proof that magic exists. We are magic. We are Black girls grown into women, growing people, and this collection of Black Girl Magicians are mantras, prayers, and promises of our survival. The anthology this portfolio comes from, *The BreakBeat Poets Volume 2: Black Girl Magic*, edited by myself, Idrissa Simmonds, and Jamila Woods, is a literary but breathing example of our great-great-great-great grandmothers' triumphant and explosive war cry.

Halcyon Kitchen

Granma cautioned in a kitchen off Century and Hoover:
Never throw your hair away. Burn it. Till yellow
cornbread bakes and greens release pot liquor,
her garnet-polished fingers unraveled each cornrow.

Never throw your hair away, burn it till yellow
flames flick up and turn orange, blue. Overhead,
her garnet-polished fingers unraveled each cornrow,
wrestling. I reminisce, standing over her deathbed.

Rain picks up and turns ocher, blue. Unsaid
were simple things. Oxtail stew and yam
recipes I recollect, standing over her deathbed.
She smoked Mores leaning in the kitchen doorjamb,

when simple things — oxtail stew and yam
recipes — were not measured nor written. Cooking while
she smoked Mores leaning in the kitchen doorjamb,
her left hand in the profound curve of her hip. She'd say, Chile,

ma recipes are not measured nor written. Cooking while
I sat alongside the stove waiting for the hot comb, meantime
her left hand in the profound curve of her hip, she'd say, Chile,
I may be dead and gone, but you mark my words. Sometimes

I sat alongside the stove waiting for the hot comb, meantime
I loved watching her smoking, cooking, talking with More fingers,
I may be dead and gone, but you'll mark my words. This time,
she is quiet. I hold maroon-polished hands as her soul lifts, waits, lingers.

I loved watching her smoking, cooking, talking with More fingers.
Halcyon rain picks up, soaks me blue. Nothing unsaid.
She is quiet. I hold maroon-polished hands as her soul lifts, waits,
    lingers,
restful. I'm remembering — standing over her deathbed.

Cardi B Tells Me about Myself

Dear Frustrated in Flatbush,
Gurl, just go on ahead then.
You waiting for your Daddy
to give you the thumbs up?
Do what you like.
Do what makes your ass happy.
They gon' call you all makes
and sizes of hoe anyway.
That's how this thing been set up.
But just cuz they name a thing a thing,
don't mean it ain't still named God
in some other language.

Your fortune cookie say you poppin'.
You a full spread of good shit.
Your rotten wisdom tooth.
Your pockmarked shoulders.
Those eyelashes ain't come here
to talk about the weather.
You the hottest day in July
and every fire hydrant in this city
is written out to your name.

Whatchu dead fish for?
Whatchu call that stroke?
Drowning? Baptism?
Gurl, you betta lick that
collection plate clean
and stop pretending you just
got off the first canoe from Heaven.
You ain't nothin but
a big bowl of sweat rice.
You wring your left thigh,
they call you Vintage JuJu.
They like, "This some kind of nightmare?"

And it's just you, smoking a blunt in the dark,
cackling like rain. Like your grandmama
at her ain't-shit husband's funeral.
Bitch, you been a woman.
This ain't new skin.
Slap some Lycra on it
and call yourself a predicament.
You ain't just somebody's meal plan.
Pull back your hair and eat.

And look at this muhfukka,
sittin across the table,
lookin like he wanna bite you.
Tonight is tonight and tomorrow
might be somewhere else,
serenading some lesser bitch.
Throw his ass a bone and
stop worrying about your credit score.

You stay banging your tambourine
to the wrong hymnal.
I'm sure they had names
and inescapable mouths but
what your ex gotta do with this?
Why you still got his body in your linen closet?
That's nasty. Bitch, keep your house clean.
You crying over spilled dick. Gurl buh-bye.
Getchu a free refill.

You too black for indie film housewife.
You too naked for conversation like this.
Too much soft brutality,
too much bathtub depression.
Why you always got your neck swung open?
Free throat don't pay for your boy's sneakers.

You already know I don't even sigh for free.
Shit, I stroke a shallow strobe light,
inchworm down 4 feet of greasy pole,
and I still don't feel like any less than a miracle.

Ode to Fetty Wap (written after strip club)

A reading from the book of Willie Maxwell 679:1738

... then Rap Gawd formed a man
from the dust of the auto-tune
&breathed into his nostrils
the breath of Rémy Martin
the man became Fetty Wap.

Rap Gawd saw fit to
make Fetty a counterpart.
so he caused the man to fall into a deep sleep;
while he was sleeping
he took one of the man's eyes
then closed up the place with flesh.
then the Rap Gawd made a woman
from the eye he had taken out of the man.

the creation story of Fetty
the first trap rapper to make a song
I might play at my wedding.

there's a choir of church mothers
smiling down on the brown boy
that sings of a woman's worth
in a culture destined to nullify it.

do you know how long
sisters been waiting
for a brother
to willingly let us hit the bando?
(after patiently explaining what the fuck that means.)

l'union fait la force
your music emblematic of the motto of Haiti
unity makes strength

as we scream **SQUAAADDDD!**
the weight of that bass
hits hard
like Gawd's tears
landing on glow in the dark floors
'cause Gawd does not just "cry"
He makes it rain
on a crowd of women
in heels higher than most GPAs
dancing their way through
nursing school
&out of some deadbeat's
roach-filled 1 bedroom.

the fellas
big brother
arm-wrapped shoulders
singing off-key
about Ki's &pies
and other shit
they have no real idea about.

the only song in the club
that allows a hetero male
to gaze into the eyes
of another
[suspected] hetero male
and/or stranger
singing his fucking heart out.

make him more mathematician
than murderer
spewing lyrics repping
the urban district's finest cognac
this

is a black man's
"Sweet Caroline"
oh, oh, oh!

Fetty, you got me —
I, too, see heaven
peering through
the pearly-gated smile
of that gap-toothed princess
in your video.

I, too, have a glock in my rari —
in the form of a master's degree
but don't get it twisted
this summa cum laude bloaw
anytime a motherfucker think
they know me!
&my trap look a lot
like a dimly-lit cafe
with semicold
red stripes
a microphone
a couple judges
but I'll be damned
if anyone tell me
I ain't a **queen of this shit**.

&then I blink
&the bass subsides
&the song fades
into another brother
caring more
about his golden grill
than making the best
of a family business.

&she picks up her ass
her purse
slides off the pole
disappears
into a mixture
of low-budget smoke machines
&catcalling men

wedding bands tangled
in the drawstring of their sweats

&another Saturday twerks
itself into the crisp breeze of Sunday morning
&the church mothers glance over the room
covered in government-issued confetti
&Gawd smiles
as they bellow in unison

"I want you to be mine again!"

BIANCA LYNNE SPRIGGS

What Women Are Made Of

There are many kinds of open.
—Audre Lorde

We are all ventricle, spine, lung, larynx, and gut.
Clavicle and nape, what lies forked in an open palm;

we are follicle and temple. We are ankle, arch,
sole. Pore and rib, pelvis and root

and tongue. We are wishbone and gland and molar
and lobe. We are hippocampus and exposed nerve

and cornea. Areola, pigment, melanin, and nails.
Varicose. Cellulite. Divining rod. Sinew and tissue,

saliva and silt. We are blood and salt, clay and aquifer.
We are breath and flame and stratosphere. Palimpsest

and bibelot and cloisonné fine lines. Marigold, hydrangea,
and dimple. Nightlight, satellite, and stubble. We are

pinnacle, plummet, dark circles, and dark matter.
A constellation of freckles and specters and miracles

and lashes. Both bent and erect, we are all give
and give back. We are volta and girder. Make an incision

in our nectary and Painted Ladies sail forth, riding the back
of a warm wind, plumed with love and things like love.

Crack us down to the marrow, and you may find us full
of cicada husks and sand dollars and salted maple taffy

weary of welding together our daydreams. All sweet tea,
razor blades, carbon, and patchwork quilts of *Good God!*

and *Lord have mercy!* Our hands remember how to turn
the earth before we do. Our intestinal fortitude? Cumulonimbus

streaked with saffron light. Our foundation? Not in our limbs
or hips; this comes first as an amen, a hallelujah, a suckling,

swaddled psalm sung at the cosmos's breast. You want to
know what women are made of? Open wide and find out.

ELIZABETH ACEVEDO

You Mean You Don't Weep at the Nail Salon?

it's the being alone, i think, the emails but not voices. dominicans be funny, the way we love to touch — every greeting a cheek kiss, a shoulder clap, a loud.

it gots to be my period, the bloating, the insurance commercial where the husband comes home after being deployed, the last of the gouda gone, the rejection letter, the acceptance letter, the empty inbox.

a dream, these days. to work at home is a privilege, i remind myself.

spend the whole fucking day flirting with screens. window, tv, computer, phone: eyes & eyes & eyes. the keys clicking, the ding of the microwave, the broadway soundtrack i share wine with in the evenings.

these are the answers, you feel me? & the impetus. the why. of when the manicurist holds my hand, making my nails a lilliputian abstract,

i close my fingers around hers, disrupting the polish, too tight i know then, too tight to hold a stranger, but she squeezes back & doesn't let go & so finally i can.

The Etymology of "CHUUCH!"

chuuch/church

[pronounced without the *r*. the *r* is the hump on our backs. too much to weigh/wait. imagine replacing the *r* with *u*. the cupping is softer. all the things it holds. it often sounds like *ahh*. round and complete. it all comes together. like home.]

1. from the renowned *amen!* meaning *let it be*. or *so it is*. or so may have it. and take into agreement. this the stamp. the let it be said and sold. the solidarity screaming from the stem of our spouts. this is the yes.

2. used in positions of *incognegro*. the screech beyond the never-lands of our blocks. posted and protecting. remember the code. often known as *i peep game*. or the never ending *i'm on it, bro*. closing the deal. the celebration of *i see you*. welcome to my memory for another day. let the house of our bodies be grateful. for our sacrifices have not killed us. yet.

3. said like a vaccine. the awkwardness dancing on your lip before your words fall and ruin the show. this can also be the broken promise. the text you know you won't reply to. the person you drag your heart for with no supplies left to clean. this is sometimes the last stake. the call of *i don't understand, but imma figure this shit out*. the choir is singing and you can't understand anything sang. you sing. for the house is still bouncing. ace boom cooling.

4. this is not to be confused with *sending off*. it's the most honest thing we are unsure of. for every house is not covered. so we cover our prayer with a *this is it. this is real* and our lives. we do not *agree* to this condition of our well-being. blast and break our cinder blocks like tambourines. we weave the stories together. thank and talk through our teeth. for *we know. we understand*. we light the sky. shake up with god and find the move. keep the key. keep it pushing.

JUSTICE AMEER

(After God Herself)

Adam ate an apple
it got stuck in his throat
and they called him Eve
the progenitor
the creator of all things
the mother of strength
and fortitude
and sadness
Adam ate an apple
choked on it so hard
a rib popped out of his chest
and they called it Eve
the progenitor
the creator of all things
the mother of strength and fortitude
and sadness
it takes the hacking of a body
to make a woman
Adam hacking up a piece of his body
it was just a piece of fruit
they called me fruit once too
they called me fruity
before they called me flaming
before they called me faggot
before they called me woman
i thought i would have
to hack this body into pieces
woman, a name stuck in my throat
right under the apple Adam tried to eat
choked on it for years
waited for my ribs to pop out
my chest to explode
for my Eve to be created
from the fruit i couldn't swallow
they called me fruit once

until they called me woman
and then they just called me fruitless
as if it took a womb to be
progenitor
creator
mother of all things
strength and fortitude and sadness
they reckon God looked
at the image of herself
and called it Adam
they still don't call me woman
they still don't birth me Eve
even though they cast me out
my throat shrunken close
with the fruit still stuck in it
like Adam
before they called him Eve
and suddenly i am a stranger
to Eden
i am a stranger to this body
as if it hadn't always been mine
i reckon God looked
at the image of herself
and called it me
but i don't know if that
was before or after the apple
before or after Adam choked
which came first
the progenitor or the mother
the apple or the rib
the strength or the sadness
this body was God's original creation
but they called it sin
they called it Adam
I reckon God looked

at the image of herself
and called Adam Eve
after she choked on his name
some fruit that bloomed
in everyone else's throat
but she could never quite swallow
the fall of man was an apple
hacked up from a fruitless body
a woman learning what evil was
like a man forcing his name upon you
the fall of man was a rib
being torn from a chest
and men calling that violence holy
naming a woman based only
on the body parts she's made of
the fall of man
was the beginning of Eve
Eve casting out Adam's name
Eve discovering who she was
the progenitor
the creator of all things
the mother of strength
and fortitude
and sadness
the fall of man
was Eve becoming a woman
with or without Eden's approval
and now
every time someone
tries to call her Adam
tries to force the apple
of his name down her throat
she laughs
she swallows

she looks at God herself
and she smiles

A sestina for a black girl who does not know how to braid hair

Your hands have no more worth than tree stumps at harvest.
Don't sit on my porch while I make myself useful.
Braid secrets in scalps on summer days for my sisters.
Secure every strand of gossip with tight rubber bands of value.
What possessed you to ever grow your nails so long?
How can you have history without braids?

A black girl is happiest when rooted to the scalp are braids.
She dances with them whipping down her back like corn in winds
    of harvest.
Braiding forces our reunions to be like the shifts your mothers work,
    long.
I find that being surrounded by only your own is more useful.
Gives our mixed blood more value.
Solidifies your place with your race, with your sisters.

Your block is a layered cake of your sisters.
Force your lips quiet and sweet and they'll speak when they need to
    practice braids.
Your hair length is the only part of you that holds value.
The tallest crop is worshipped at harvest.
So many little hands in your head. You are finally useful.
Your hair is yours, your hair is theirs, your hair is, for a black girl, long.

Tender-headed ass won't last 'round here long.
Cut your nails and use your fists to protect yourself against your
    sisters.
Somehow mold those hands useful.
You hair won't get pulled in fights if they are in braids.
Beat out the weak parts of the crops during harvest.
When they are limp and without soul they have value.

If you won't braid or defend yourself what is your value?
Sitting on the porch until dark sweeps in needing to be invited,
    you'll be needing long.

When the crop is already used what is its worth after harvest?
You'll learn that you can't ever trust those quick to call themselves
    your sisters.
They yearn for the gold that is your braids.
You hold on your shoulders a coveted item that is useful.

Your presence will someday become useful.
One day the rest of your body will stagger under the weight of its
    value.
Until then, sit in silence in the front with your scalp on fire from
    the braids.
I promise you won't need anyone too long.
One day you will love yourself on your own, without the validation
    of sisters.
No longer a stump wailing for affection at harvest.

ARACELIS GIRMAY

sister was the wolf

sister was the wolf
& could cross easily through

the mountain dark to den
keen & quivered with

the muscular siege of slit   purse
purple with hours

purse purple with birthwork
her sight both inward-

& outward-lit
on what small sparkle of pyrite

in the silt or the thick smell of her own
wilderness opening shit & hair & blood

each little birth
an astonishment of form

inside its own tiny veil
licked toward the air of this Other Side

[*Live!*]

then that sound
from the hospital's infant table

after what seemed like years
of silence   a mew

which held inside it

all the voices of

this dream & other animals
trying to begin

Flight

I call to ask my mother the name of the street where we bought the
     suitcases when we left
Brooklyn. A better question would have been how did it feel to be
     sliced from the rib of Pine and
Loring and sent, like a kite, up North. Or tell me what your mother
     said to you in her grand rear
room the night we left, seated on the edge of her bed in her night-
     gown, muted in the low light.
So many bellies in the house. Cacophony of kreyol and Brooklyn
     buk and sweet sweat across the
walls. Did she tell you to follow your husband. Did she tell you
     anything about us. How, above
all, you should keep us anchored to here, where the distance between
     comfort and safety is
measurable by the length of the hallway, the distance from one
     room to the next. The rooms, like
capsules, each with its own medicine for Black kids. Or, tell me
     what you wore on the plane
ride. I only remember what I wore: stockings and Mary Janes and
     the pink knit pleated skirt. I did
not remember this was your first time flying, a grown woman over
     thirty, and you had never seen
how small the world looked beneath your feet.

SNOW CITY ARTS

ERIC ELSHTAIN
───────────────

Introduction

Snow City Arts provides one-on-one instruction in the visual arts,
creative writing, music, theater, and media arts to pediatric patients
at four Chicagoland hospitals. Over the last twenty years, we have
taught sixteen thousand students and have led more than fifty thousand art workshops.

When a Snow City Arts teaching artist knocks on a door and is
invited into a potential student's hospital room, the teaching artist
needs to find the right catalyst as soon as they can. They never know
how much time they are going to have with a student, so they jump
right in, working under the philsophy that in art a student learns best
by doing, working in "yes... and" relationships with the teaching
artist. No matter what form of art inspires the student, whether it
be painting, photography, music, film, or theater, they are exposed
to a variety of art-making materials, learning basic to more advanced
techniques and practices through studio-based pedagogy.

Students often do their work through their discomforts and pains,
anxieties and exhaustions. Whatever the media, we are consistently
amazed at the artworks born out of the chaos and discomfort of the
students' circumstances. That said, we consider the art and poetry
not as the work of the "sick" but as the work of serious artistic ex-
plorers and apprentices, novices and experts. In this small portfolio,
we have paired poems with visual art. The conversation created between these two mediums symbolizes the multitude of conversations
between teaching artist and student artist that have been, and contin-
ue to be, the impetuses for the now tens of thousands of art-making
encounters we have had the pleasure of facilitating since 1998, when
the first teaching artist — a poet — stepped into a room at Rush
University Children's Hospital and asked, "Would you like to make
some art with me?"

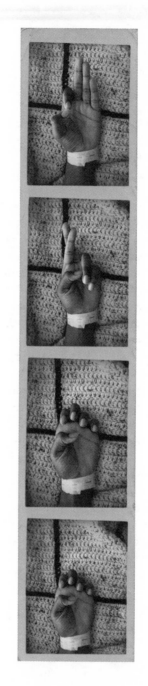

Free, by Jaiden, age ten.

FRANCISCO

From "Burglar's Got Your Tongue"

Homer doesn't speak.
He can speak, occasionally doing so in his sleep,
but he doesn't with intent.
Homer's therapist, after diagnosing him with "elective mutism,"
recommended he be enrolled in music and learn an instrument.
Homer's parents were excited for their son to learn an instrument.
They romanticized the notion of their inexplicably mute son being
    a musical genius
communicating not through words, but the soul.
In reality, he was a cacophonous mess and their new weekend alarm
    clock.
Homer, a fan of the trumpet and annoying his parents, was often
    asked to practice outside.
This suited him just fine ...

—Age twenty

Flowerheart Red, by Rin, age sixteen.

The Love

After "[Love is a purple angel]" by Hoa Nguyen

The heart
is a skinny
piece of paper.
Half purple. Half
pink.
With 2 googly
eyes that shake.
With a glittery mouth
that's the color of a
rainbow.
With 2 wavy arms
and 2 wavy legs
wiggling everywhere.
With curly hair
as curly as a
chair.
This heart
is the heart
of somebody in love.

—*Age eleven*

Monklionworbutterfly, by Jamari, age eleven.

Animals with Feelings

Happiness is a blue fish eating

Sadness is an orange turtle trapped in a fish tank

Anger is a yellow lion hunting animals to eat

Kindness is a red snake sharing food

Trust is a gray tiger telling the truth

— Age nine

Sunrise, by Gabriella, age twenty.

I Can't Stand Watches

I don't understand how watches tell time — I think time is tricky
I can't stop it and it doesn't stop for no one; therefore, time is tricky
I never knew anything is infinite
I figured out that one thing was: *time*: it tricky
every second that passes is a new one, is it the future
or the past... I could never figure it out... time is tricky
to review and view things are completely different
to view is present to review is past that's what I don't get, time is
    tricky
past is gone present is now future is present
that makes Montarius wonder why time is tricky

— Age eighteen

ELIZABETH ACEVEDO* is the daughter of Dominican immigrants. She is a National Poetry Slam Champion. *The Poet X* (HarperCollins, 2018) is her debut novel.

KAZIM ALI's most recent collection of poetry is *Inquisition* (Wesleyan University Press, 2018) and his most recent prose book is *Silver Road: Essays, Maps & Calligraphies* (Tupelo Press, 2018).

JUSTICE AMEER* is a Black poet and organizer based in Providence, Rhode Island. Xe is a Pink Door fellow and one of the inaugural Feminine Empowerment Movement (FEM) Slam Champions.

ELLEN BASS's* most recent book is *Like a Beggar* (Copper Canyon Press, 2014). A chancellor of the Academy of American Poets, she teaches in Pacific University's MFA program.

SHERWIN BITSUI* (Diné) is the author of *Flood Song* (Copper Canyon Press, 2009) and *Shapeshift* (University of Arizona Press, 2003). He teaches at the Institute of American Indian Arts.

MAHOGANY L. BROWNE is coeditor of *The BreakBeat Poets Volume 2: Black Girl Magic* (Haymarket Books, 2018) and author of *Black Girl Magic* (Roaring Brook Press, 2018) and *Redbone* (Willow Books, 2015).

SARAH BROWNING is author of *Killing Summer* (Sibling Rivalry Press, 2017), cofounder and executive director of Split This Rock, and associate fellow of the Institute for Policy Studies.

KWAME DAWES is the author of twenty-one books of poetry, most recently *City of Bones: A Testament* (Northwestern University Press, 2017), and is a chancellor of the Academy of American Poets.

CAMILLE T. DUNGY's most recent books are *Trophic Cascade* (Wesleyan University Press, 2017) and *Guidebook to Relative Strangers: Journeys into Race, Motherhood, and History* (W.W. Norton, 2017).

ERIC ELSHTAIN* has worked as a teaching artist for Snow City Arts since 2005. He edits Beard of Bees Press and his poetry book is *This Thin Memory A-ha* (Verge Books, 2014).

FRANCISCO'S* piece is an excerpt from a much longer story that is still a work-in-progress.

GABRIELLA'S* piece is inspired by the work of Josef Albers.

ARACELIS GIRMAY is the author of the poetry collections *The Black Maria* (2016) and *Kingdom Animalia* (2011), both from BOA Editions, as well as *Teeth* (Curbstone Press, 2007).

EBONI HOGAN* is the 2012 Women of the World Poetry Slam Champion and her plays have been featured at the National Black Theater, the Living Theater, and elsewhere.

RAYCH JACKSON* currently teaches fourth grade in the Chicago Public School system. She is the 2017 NUPIC Champion and is working on her debut collection of poems.

JAIDEN* participated in a project called Positive Language that uses ASL and photography.

JAMARI* invented a new animal using nineteenth-century lithographs to make the collage that appears in this issue.

KIANDRA JIMENEZ* holds an MFA from Antioch University. She teaches poetry and fiction at Yavapai College, and splits her heart between poems and gardening.

ILYA KAMINSKY is the author of *Deaf Republic* (Graywolf Press, 2019) and *Dancing in Odessa* (Tupelo Press, 2004), and is coeditor of the *Ecco Anthology of International Poetry* (Ecco Press, 2010).

E'MON LAUREN* was named Chicago's first Youth Poet Laureate and uses poetry and playwriting to explore a philosophy of hood womanism. Her poem in the issue is from her first chapbook, *Commando* (Haymarket Books, 2017).

LEONEL* was practicing his knowledge of metaphor in his poem.

ROYA MARSH* is the poet in residence with Urban Word NYC and works feverishly toward LGBTQIA justice and dismantling white supremacy.

MONTARIUS* was imitating Urdu ghazals in his poem in this issue.

SHARON OLDS is, most recently, the author of *Odes* (Knopf, 2016) and *Stag's Leap* (Knopf, 2012), for which she received the Pulitzer Prize and the T.S. Eliot Prize.

RIN* was working on silkscreen in their piece in this issue.

SONIA SANCHEZ* is one of the most important writers of the Black Arts Movement. The author of sixteen books, she has received the Robert Frost Medal and the Robert Creeley Award.

SHANI's* poem in this issue was influenced by the playful comparisons in Hoa Nguyen's poem.

SOLMAZ SHARIF is the author of *Look* (Graywolf Press, 2016). She is a lecturer at Stanford University.

TERISA SIAGATONU* is an award-winning poet, arts educator, and community organizer born and rooted in the Bay Area.

IDRISSA SIMMONDS* is a poet, essayist, and fiction writer at work on her first novel.

BIANCA LYNNE SPRIGGS* is the author of *Call Her by Her Name* (Northwestern University Press, 2016) and *The Galaxy Is a Dance Floor* (Argos Books, 2016).

PAUL TRAN* is the first Asian American since 1993 to win the Nuyorican Poets Café Grand Slam. Their work appears or is forthcoming in the *New Yorker* and elsewhere.

JAVIER ZAMORA recently received a Lannan Foundation fellowship. His first book is *Unaccompanied* (Copper Canyon Press, 2017).

* First appearance in *Poetry*.

POETRY FOUNDATION
APRIL FEATURES

POETRY PODCASTS	***POETRY MAGAZINE PODCAST*** *Poetry* editors **Don Share** and **Lindsay Garbutt** talk to contributors and share their poem selections from this issue with listeners. ***POETRY OFF THE SHELF*** Listen to Poetry Off the Shelf's ***A Change of World***, our six-part special series devoted to the intersections between poetry and the women's movement. ***POETRYNOW*** April's four-minute episodes feature new poems by **Diana Arterian, Randall Horton, Prageeta Sharma, Roberto Harrison**, and **Feliz Lucia Molina**. Produced in partnership with the WFMT Radio Network. Podcasts are available free from the iTunes store and on poetryfoundation.org.
HARRIET BLOG	To celebrate National Poetry Month, *Harriet* will publish a new essay each day by previously featured bloggers.
POETRY FOUNDATION .ORG	Find essays, interviews, and a new animated series of contemporary poems retold as short films for all ages created in partnership with **Motionpoems**. And whether you are a teacher, student, parent, or autodidact, check out our new **Learn Area**.
EVENTS	Plan your trip to Chicago to see some of our April events! *Poetry off the Shelf* **DAVID BIESPIEL, WENDY WILLIS & ELIZABETH TAYLOR** Thursday, April 5, 7:00 PM Poetry Foundation *Poetry & Music* **KAY RYAN & THE APOLLO CHORUS SALON CONCERT & CONVERSATION** Thursday, April 12, 7:00 PM Poetry Foundation *Poetry off the Shelf* **LINGUA FRANCA: SOUTH AFRICAN SPOKEN WORD COMPANY** Wednesday, April 18, 7:00 PM Poetry Foundation
EXHIBITION	***Bettissima:* Treasures from the Poets House Elizabeth Kray Archives** April 3 – May 30, 2018 Monday – Friday, 11:00 AM – 4:00 PM

POETRY FOUNDATION
61 West Superior Steet
Chicago, Illinois 60654
poetryfoundation.org

POETRY

Podcast: Pyramid
Scheme

THE EDITORS

New poems by Tim Upperton,
Anahera Gildea, Hera Lindsay Bird,
and Murray Edmond.

Editors Lindsay Garbutt and Don
Share go inside the pages of
POETRY, talking to poets and critics,
debating the issues, and sharing
their poem selections with listeners.

poetryfoundation.org

PODCAST

P|O
E|T
R|Y
FOUNDATION

THE frost place

Conference on Poetry and Teaching | June 23 - 26, 2018
Director: Dawn Potter, **Associate Director:** Kerrin McCadden
Faculty: Diana Goetsch, Joaquín Zihuatanejo

+Writing Intensive | June 27 - 28, 2018
Workshop Leader: Kamilah Aisha Moon

Conference on Poetry | July 8 - 14, 2018
Director: Martha Rhodes, **Faculty:** Maudelle Driskell, Vievee Francis,
Kevin Prufer, Jason Schneiderman, Connie Voisine
Poetry Fellows: Ben Purkert, Phillip Williams

Poetry Seminar | July 29 - August 3, 2018
Director: Patrick Donnelly, **Faculty:** Martha Collins, Eduardo C. Corral

frostplace.org | frost@frostplace.org | (603) 823-5510

Carl Dennis
Night School
The poems in Carl Dennis's thirteenth collection are informed by an engagement with a world not fully accessible to the light of day, a world that can only be known with help from the imagination.
Penguin • 112 pp. • 978-0-14-313235-6 • $20.00

Carol Muske-Dukes
Blue Rose
"Every image and abutment, every syllable and turn of diction earns its place in the cadence of the whole. These poems arrive like a lifeline."— Linda Gregerson
Penguin • 80 pp. • 978-0-14-313125-0 • $18.00

sam sax
Madness
An "astounding" (Terrance Hayes) debut collection of poems exposing the links between desire, addiction, and the history of mental health. Winner of the 2016 National Poetry Series Competition.
Penguin • 96 pp. • 978-0-14-313170-0 • $18.00

Yrsa Daley-Ward
bone
Foreword by Kiese Laymon
The poems in Yrsa Daley-Ward's collection, *bone*, are exactly that: reflections on a particular life honed to their essence—so clear and pared-down, they become universal.
Penguin • 160 pp. • 978-0-14-313261-5 • $15.00

William Logan
Rift of Light
Logan's eleventh collection is a master class of powerful feeling embedded in language. Ranging from Martin Luther to an abandoned crow, from a midwife toad to a small-town janitor, Logan shows an encyclopedic attention to the passing world.
Penguin • 112 pp. • 978-0-14-313182-3 • $18.00

Pattiann Rogers
Quickening Fields
Fifty-three poems that focus on the wide variety of life-forms present on earth and their unceasing zeal to exist, their constant "push against the beyond" and the human experience among these lives. "These poems fill a primordial urge of verse: to express awe at the world."—*Publishers Weekly*.
Penguin • 128 pp. • 978-0-14-313132-8 • $20.00

Debora Greger
In Darwin's Room
An artful new collection from a poet who sees the extraordinary within the everyday. "An exemplary Greger poem occurs to the ear as a striking painting does to the eye: the particulars of its composition emerge only after the first thrill of the whole."— *The Harvard Review*.
Penguin • 128 pp. • 978-0-14-313131-1 • $18.00

Mary Oliver
Devotions
The Selected Poems of Mary Oliver
Penguin Press • 480 pp. • 978-0-399-56324-9 • $30.00

REVOLUTIONS is a unique collaboration between poet JOHN MATTHIAS, printmaker JEAN DIBBLE, and critic ROBERT ARCHAMBEAU.

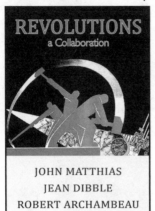

JOHN MATTHIAS has published some thirty books of poetry, translation, criticism, and scholarship.

JEAN DIBBLE is a printmaker and painter who has exhibited extensively, both internationally and nationally.

ROBERT ARCHAMBEAU is a poet & literary critic. He teaches English at Lake Forest College.

Two poetic sequences by Matthias, "The HIJ" and "After Five Words Englished from the Russian" generate, first, a corresponding sequence of poster-poems by Dibble and, second, a series of "free commentaries" by Archambeau. "The HIJ," emerging initially from an alphabetical game using chance operations in the Dictionary, eventually produces something of a character and a narrative, both of which are probed by the artist and commentator. The "Five Words" are translated from Russian poet Osip Mandelstam's "He Who Finds a Horseshoe." Again, the poster-poems enlarge on the text and the commentaries complete a sequence of revolutions without resolutions.

"How to write in the time of Trump and Putin? In words and images, John Matthias, Jean Dibble, and Robert Archambeau give you an answer to consider: find the muse of amusement and the reality of facts and twin them: you will arrive at "Revolutions," which instructs us on the possible meanings and uses of poetry in an Age of Emergency. There is much consolation in the anxiety of forms."
—Maxine Chernoff

DOS MADRES
www.dosmadres.com

REVOLUTIONS - a Collaboration
ISBN: 978-1-939929-74-7
126 pages, 9"x 6" $20.00 U.S.
First Published: April 2017
by Dos Madres Press, Inc.

CONTACT: editor@dosmadres.com
You may order books directly from Dos Madres Press, Inc. at:
http://www.dosmadres.com

Subscribe to POETRY today and receive a free tote!

Print subscription comes with complimentary digital access.

poetryfoundation.org/subscribe

Hearing That Joe Arroyo Song at Ibiza Nightclub, 2008

A boy I did not marry   taught me to dance salsa on 2   placed
the fingers of his left hand   on my untutored spine;   you know what
it's like to become someone's clave

to love for the span   of the trombone's long breath   he   whispered
negra so I spun   my heart landing   on   the   rum-covered   linoleum
of a nightclub

on what used to be New York Ave   in what used to be Chocolate City
I let him turn & spin   my name   *bella negra*
          his hands were less tender but still I let them roam

          when I   *1, 2, 3*   *5, 6, 7*   in front of my mirror
I was always la negra defended in the lyric   and   you   can   forgive
searching hands when a mouth swells the biggest ache of your body

                              into song

Moana Means Home: A Contrapuntal

The team behind Moana has taken great care to respect the cultures of the Pacific Islands that inspired the film, and we regret that the Maui costume has offended some.

— *Disney, Inc.*

someone will	always want	my skin.
touch the Earth	to take	what's mine.
once, I wanted	a white girl's skin	more than
my own soil.	I cried so hard,	an ocean
tried to drown my ankles	until I became a boat	floating above myself
in myself.	I never want to be lost	at sea
again. Daughter of Oceania	at high tide. Daughter of	open-mouthed Sun
wanting me home.	Ancestor's language tatted	on my body.
my skin is sacred ground.	on my skin	my story will breathe.

*By Elizabeth Acevedo